Masks

Contents

Many Masks

Masks are used for many different purposes. Sometimes they are used for protection. Sometimes actors wear them. Sometimes they are worn for fun!

Masks at Work

Some people wear masks at work.
The masks protect their eyes and faces.
Some masks even clean the air that
people breathe.

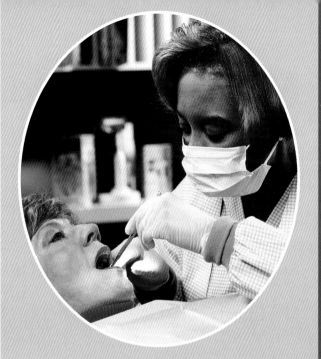

Sometimes firefighters
need to wear masks.
The masks help them
breathe when there
is a lot of smoke
in the air.

Sometimes dentists
wear masks. A mask
protects the patient
and the dentist
from germs.

Masks on Stage

Sometimes actors wear masks. A mask helps an actor look like someone or something else. A mask can also show a character's feelings.

Masks for Sports

Masks provide important protection in some sports. Sometimes a mask is part of a helmet.

Masks Under Water

Divers wear masks that help them see under the water. The masks are made so that no water can get inside.

Masks for Celebrations

People often wear masks for special events or celebrations. This happens all around the world.

Make Your Own Mask

You will need:

- a balloon
- paper, torn into pieces
- paste
- piece of elastic
- stapler
- paints and brushes
- decorations

What to do:

1 Blow up the balloon. Draw eyes and a mouth on it.

2 Paste pieces of paper on one side of the balloon. Don't cover the eyes and mouth. Build up several layers of paper.

3 When the paper is
dry, burst the balloon.

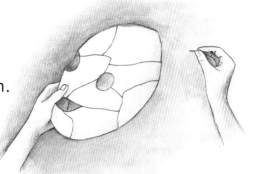

4 Staple a piece of
elastic to both sides
of the mask.

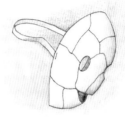

5 Paint and decorate
your mask.

15

Index